RIGHTS

Pictured: Jules Dalou's Wisdom Supporting Liberty.
Athena, the goddess of wisdom,
is supporting Liberty, the goddess of freedom.
Quote paraphrases John F. Kennedy[1].
Design copyright Inspirationz Inc. Ltd.
Artwork by Ira Paniukova.

RIGHTS

REDISCOVERING OUR MEANS TO LIBERTY

TERRY VERHOEVEN

RIGHTS INSTITUTE
Championing Moral Space

RIGHTS

Print: 978-0-473-50332-1
ePUB: 978-0-473-50333-8
MOBI: 978-0-473-50334-5
PDF: 978-0-473-50335-2

Rights Institute
P.O. Box 9547
Newmarket
Auckland 1149
New Zealand
Phone +64(21)837472
www.rightsinstitute.com

To all men who are not woke, but awake

www.rightsinstitute.org

"God grant, that not only the Love of Liberty,
but a thorough Knowledge of the Rights of Man,
may pervade all the Nations of the Earth, so that a
Philosopher may set his Foot anywhere on its Surface,
and say, 'This is my Country'."

**Benjamin Franklin, in a Letter to David Hartley
dated December 4, 1789; reported in
Albert H. Smyth, ed., *The Writings of Benjamin
Franklin* (1907), Volume 10, p72**

CONTENTS

INTRODUCTION

"Their own confession of guilt lies in their terminology. Why do they use the word 'rights' to denote the things they are advocating? Why don't they preach what they practice? Why don't they name it openly and attempt to justify it, if they can? The answer is obvious."

Ayn Rand, Essay "Collectivized 'Rights'" (June 1963),
The Virtue of Selfishness, **Chapter 14, p124**

Today, few people can coherently argue for rights: what they are, why they are needed, who has them, and how. Most people's understanding of rights is that they are had by majority vote, or by virtue of possessing the human genome, or by the decree of some appointed authority such as the United Nations, the Founding Fathers, or Scripture. This critical lack of understanding is why rights are being abrogated the world over in the name of "rights," and why that abrogation is being met with popular support rather than moral outrage, fierce resistance, and convincing argument.

The fact is that rights are gained by reasoning. Rights result from reason identifying its own existential needs in a social context. It is because of a lack of reasoning, and of reasoned self-awareness specifically, that populaces are trading away their rights for privileges misnamed as "rights."

The aim of this treatise is to engage your reason, and bring an objective understanding of rights within your reach so that you can, with a bit of effort, grasp what rights actually are, then use your new-found knowledge to defend not only your rights, but the very institution of rights.

Getting straight to the point: A skeleton definition of rights is that **a *right* is a moral principle defining and sanctioning a man's freedom of action in a social context.**[2] In the pages that follow, this definition is expanded upon, and several concepts to do with rights are introduced. These include: man, who is the subject and beneficiary of rights; moral space, which rights define and maximize; autonomy and liberty, which are the personal enjoyment of moral space and the universal enjoyment of autonomy, respectively; agape or good-willed reasoning, which is the ethos needed to be fit for liberty and for liberty to work; immorality, amorality, and privilege, which are three corollaries of any rights violation (the last, privilege, when the violation is sanctioned by law); the nature of rights, including the five stages of realizing rights; compossibility, which is a litmus test for the legitimacy of any set of asserted rights; a proper epistemology of rights, which differentiates between needing rights, having rights in mind, and enjoying rights; rights-recognition, which is the judicial application of rights; property, the right to which is the only means of implementing rights compossibly; and finally, individual rights versus collective "rights," which are the concept and anti-concept of rights respectively.

Let's begin…

1. THE RIGHTS OF *MAN*

"In the name of the values that keep you alive,
do not let your vision of man be distorted by the ugly, the cowardly,
the mindless in those who have never achieved his title."
Ayn Rand, *Atlas Shrugged* (1957), p979

Ever since the World Wars of the last century, so-called human rights have been usurping the Rights of Man. Here, the sense of "man" has nothing to do with gender; it has to do with a particular ability – an ability not all humans have.

Losing the essential meaning of "man" has brought about the loss of the proper meaning of rights; it has brought about the loss because rights pertain to the "man" in "human," not to humans per se. If rights are to be resurrected, *man* needs to be resurrected first. It is only by being a man, or in the process of becoming or developing into a man, that a human (i.e., a possessor of the human genome) comes within the purview of rights.

So, what is a man?

During the Enlightenment, when rights were being discovered, for-mulated, and institutionalized, a man was defined as "a creature endued with reason,"[3] where a creature was defined as "a living being," that is, an integration of biological matter and consciousness. This was a variant of Aristotle's 2,400-year-old definition of man as "the rational animal."[4] Both definitions are genderless. Both recognize that the essence of man is neither a genome nor a gender, but the ability to make rational choices. This presupposes a specific type of consciousness: one that can abstract, form concepts, and apprehend reality by a process of reason.

Consistent with all of the above, the word "man" derives from the Old English verb *man*, which, according to Francis Henry Stratmann's and Henry Bradley's *A Middle English Dictionary* (1891), means "have in mind, think," from the Proto-Indo-European root *men-* "to think," whence the words mental, mentor, and mind come. In other words, man is the thinker; he and she is the reasonable creature in that word's original sense: able to reason. It is no coincidence that the verbs manumit and emancipate also have "man" as their root; being able to think and reason, and being fit for freedom, go hand in hand.

Our Age of Unenlightenment is epitomized nowhere more so than in those who identify themselves as being "woke" (a word that originally meant "weak or feeble; lacking strength, might, or energy")[5] while arguing against words having "man" in them to denote the female gender. What the just-woke fail to grasp is that "woman" denotes a specific type of living being able to reason – a man with a womb (from Middle English "womman," an abbreviation of womb-man, itself an improvement on earlier "wifman," i.e., wife-man) – and that to drop "man" from "woman" is to drop reasonability from her identity.

Only human beings with the potential or capacity to reason need or are even able to exercise rights. Those who rely on their own reason to survive and flourish need and exercise rights to protect their identity as men from the folly of the unreasonable, that is, from those who are unable or unwilling to reason. Unreasonable and anti-reasoning humans who deal with others by coercion rather than persuasion need something very different to rights to protect their folly: *they* need privileges. Rights empower and protect reasonableness. Privileges empower and protect unreasonableness. More on this later.

Not all humans can reason, such as newborns and the severely mentally impaired. These have the *hue* of being man, but without the ability and will to reason, a hu(e)man is not a man, the "creature endued with reason." Human beings who are not yet or no longer men still have the right by virtue of their potential to become men, to become men. That right, which is the most fundamental right, is better known as the right to life, but really it is the right to realize the life of a man, and ideally, to pursue a moral and therewith happy life. That realization can only be made by choice, and it is that choice that every human being with the potential or capacity to reason has a right to, unless forfeited by their own criminal action.

To summarize, being human is not synonymous with being man. All men are humans, but not all humans are men. The takeaway point from this chapter is that the proper definition of "man" is "a living being endued with reason" and that rights pertain to individual men – both actual and potential – and not to the human species as such.[6]

2. MORAL SPACE

"The reason basic rights are negative is that their function is to provide
persons with a sphere of moral jurisdiction. This is due them because of their
moral nature, because they have moral tasks in life that they ought to fulfil.
Intruding on their sphere of moral jurisdiction would amount to thwarting
their moral agency. And basic rights spell out where the conduct of others
would or would not amount to intrusion."
Tibor Machan, "Rights as social guidelines,"
***Classical Individualism*, p122**

In the last chapter, we learned how rights are rooted in reason, the defining attribute of man. To divorce rights from reason is to sunder rights from the very thing by which they are gained, and from what they are meant to protect.

Rights are a principled recognition of the fact that to live and function as men in society, we each need moral space to discover, pursue, produce, acquire, enjoy, dispose of and defend our values using our reason.

Moral space, a term coined by Harvard professor Robert Nozick, denotes the sphere of moral jurisdiction in which men are free to reason and act on their reasoning. Members of a free society recognize, maximize and respect every other member's moral space by adhering to the non-initiation of force principle, also called the principle of mutual non-interference or non-aggression.

The concept of moral space recognizes that the only thing that can stop a man from reasoning or acting on reason, other than a voluntary renouncement of reason or a bout of insanity, is initiation of force, and so it is *that* that must be outlawed.

Having moral space means having freedom to deliberate and choose between right and wrong, between good and evil, and to act on and take responsibility for one's choices, limited only by the requirement that everyone else enjoy the same freedom. Moral space is the essential condition of existence required by a man for his or her survival in society. Without moral space, a human being cannot live as a man.

When they are correctly identified and properly formulated, *rights define and maximize moral space*, and in so doing, preserve the identity of man – the living being who reasons – in a social context.

To quote a woman once called the most courageous man in America, "The concept of a 'right' pertains only to action – specifically, to freedom of action. It means freedom from physical compulsion, coercion or interference by other men."[7]

Contrary to what many people believe, forcing individuals to comply with moral strictures does not make them or the one doing the forcing moral. No. Coercion is immoral, and causes others to act amorally. Initiation of force causes the one being coerced to become amoral because it prevents them from reasoning and acting on their reasoning, from making choices and taking responsibility for their choices. As Voltaire observed: "Virtue supposes liberty, as the carrying of a burden supposes active force. Under coercion there is no virtue."[8] The very notion of morality presupposes freedom of choice. Without the freedom to choose right courses of action and reject wrong courses of action – without moral space - there can be no morality.

Morality imposed at the point of a gun, and by legislation specifically, is a contradiction in terms. When one is denied the possibility of reasoning and acting on one's reasoning, of choosing between right and wrong in the pursuit of one's values, or even of having values of one's own, amorality results because of a lack of moral space.

Initiation of force (including fraud, which is an indirect use of force that denies consent) is always immoral because it is diametrically opposed to what makes a man a man: exercising a volitional consciousness. Exercising a volitional consciousness means making rational choices, or else defaulting on that responsibility, the choices and consequences being one's own to make and bear.

The only way to deny a person moral space is to initiate or threaten to initiate force against them. Initiating or threatening to initiate force against a person enlarges the perpetrator's immoral space at the price of their victims' moral space. This is the same whether the forceful aggression is initiated or threatened by an individual, a group, or government – the latter being defined as a group of individuals entrusted with or having usurped a monopoly on the legal use of force.

To summarize, rights maximize moral space mutualistically by forbidding initiation of force. In so doing, they serve to ensure that there are no obstacles to the moral actions of individual members of a society.

IMMORAL/AMORAL vs MORAL SPACE

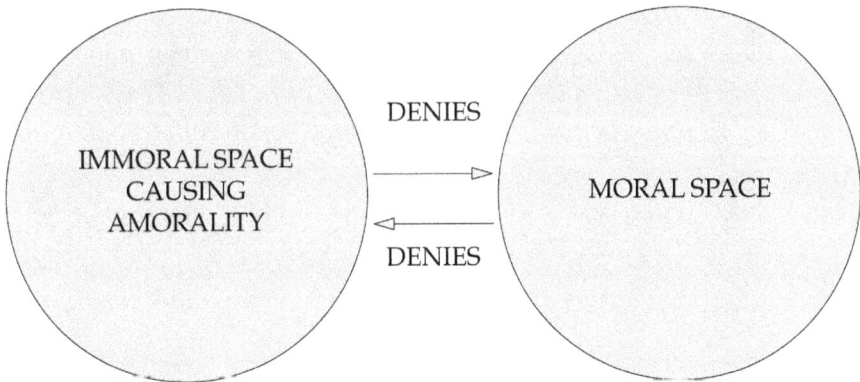

DENIES

IMMORAL SPACE
CAUSING
AMORALITY

MORAL SPACE

DENIES

3. AGAPE AND THE HISTORICAL MANDATE FOR LIBERTY

"[The] Bible is the best book in the World.
It contains more of my little Phylosophy than all the Libraries I have Seen."
John Adams, Letter to Thomas Jefferson,
25 December 1813

"To the corruptions of Christianity I am indeed opposed;
but not to the genuine precepts of Jesus himself.
I am a Christian, in the only sense he wished any one to be;
sincerely attached to his doctrines, in preference to all others;
ascribing to himself every human excellence; &
believing he never claimed any other."
Thomas Jefferson, Letter to Benjamin Rush,
April 21, 1803

John Locke, the father of Liberalism, observed that "The end of law is not to abolish or restrain, but to preserve and enlarge freedom."[9] Freedom in the context of rights means the freedom to be moral, or, if one so chooses, to be immoral, provided one's actions do not violate anyone's rights. The freedom to be moral or not, to be good or not, and to reap the reward or pay the price of one's choices and actions is, in the context of rights, a moral absolute. That moral absolute neither dictates what moral behavior is, nor gives one license to engage in immoral behaviour free from consequence; what it does is to delineate the sphere in which moral action is possible. How rights-holders ought to exercise their rights so as to be moral is outside the scope of this treatise.

Having free rein to self-direct the course of one's own life, limited only by the condition that others have the same undiminished right, is called autonomy. A state of universal autonomy is called liberty.

Whereas Renaissance thinkers in the fifteenth and sixteenth centuries identified freedom as "nature's greatest boon,"[10] Enlightenment thinkers in the eighteenth and nineteenth centuries identified liberty as mankind's most remarkable achievement, and worked assiduously to realize it.

A concise formulation of the concept of liberty was not recorded for the first time in the Enlightenment though, or even in the Renaissance for that matter. Surprisingly, or perhaps not so surprisingly, the earliest formulation is found in Scripture. Yes, Scripture. Two thousand years ago, Scripture mandated liberty.

Claiming that Scripture mandated liberty may seem out of place here, but a formulation and prescription for liberty is right there in the biblical text, as evinced below. Rest assured, this is the only chapter that deals with Scripture, a book that became the second historical pillar of a liberty-bearing Western civilization after freethinkers understood its liberating message (ancient Greek philosophy - Aristotle's Laws of Thought specifically - is the first pillar).

Before identifying where a mandate and succinct formulation of the concept of liberty is in the biblical text, it behooves us to first note how the New Testament prescribes the ethos needed for one to be fit for liberty. The ethos taught throughout the New Testament is good-willed reasoning (e.g., Matthew 22:39–40, Mark 12:31, John 13:34 and 15:12, Romans 13:9, 2 John 1:5). Good-willed reasoning is what makes individuals, and by extension a society – which is but a group of individuals – fit for liberty. The ethos of good-willed reasoning is denoted in the biblical text by the Ancient Greek verb agapeo (ἀγαπάω), which is translated in

English bibles as "to love." *Strong's Concordance* clarifies just what type of love is meant by agapeo, defining it as "wish well to" and "the love of reason," hence good-willed reasoning.

Agape or good-willed reasoning contrasts with another type of "love" in the biblical text: phileo (φιλέω), which *Strong's Concordance* defines as "personal attachment, as a matter of sentiment or feeling; while agapao is wider, embracing especially the judgment and the deliberate assent of the will as a matter of principle, duty and propriety: the two thus stand related very much as ethelo [*viz* wishing] and boulomai [*viz* determination], or as thumos [*viz* passion] and nous [*viz* understanding] respectively; the former being chiefly of the heart and the latter of the head."

And so, phileo is all about feeling (note the phonetic similarity), including wanting, desiring, and wishing. Philos means fond(ness) of, and carries the connotation of indulgent in and foolish about. Agapeo on the other hand is all about using one's 'cap' or head, including having a firm resolve, planning carefully, and understanding with the mind, with reason guiding one's good intentions.

In short, whereas phileo is soft love, agape is tough love. Hence why "the Lord disciplines the one he loves ["agape"], and chastises every son whom he receives" (Hebrews 12:6). Scripture states in no uncertain terms that agape is to love "with all your understanding" (Mark 12:33).

Throughout the gospels, Jesus advocates, practices, and teaches agape while disparaging and condemning philos. He explicitly associates the latter type of "love" with hypocrites (Matthew 6:5), the unworthy (Matthew 10:37), the haughty (Matthew 23:6), betrayers (Mark 14:44, Matthew 26:48), the sick (John 11:3), those who will lose their lives (John 12:25), and all kinds of evil (1 Timothy 6:10). There is even an exchange that takes place between Jesus and Simon Peter in chapter 21 of the book of John that has the purpose of highlighting the difference between agape and philos, the lesson of which is altogether lost in English translations. When John writes that "God is love" (1 John 4:8), agape is the word he uses for love, not philos.

Again, agape or good-willed reasoning is the ethos needed for liberty to work, both personally and for society as a whole. Agape is the prerequisite for and driving force behind liberty, while liberty is the telos or aim of agape. Liberty without agape is always in peril, and agape without liberty is always in vain.

Now, it must be noted here that it is not for anyone to decide when or whether a society is fit for liberty; fitness comes about when the good-willed reasoning of men discovers and institute rights, thereby setting their society at liberty. The point is this: the fitness – agape – comes first, and when it is lost and replaced by philos, or worse, ill-will, a loss of liberty inevitably follows.

After hammering home the importance of agape, and reiterating the Old Testament precepts that imply the right to life and property (Matthew 19:17-18, Mark 10:19, Luke 18:20, Romans 13:9), and intimating that only those who practice good-willed reasoning are fit for liberty (Galatians 5:13, 1 Peter 2:16–17), in the very last chapter of the New Testament a final precept is issued as a prelude to Judgment. That final precept, which is given immediately prior to the epilogue, is this: "Do not seal up the words of the prophecy of this scroll, because the time is near. Let the one who does wrong continue to do wrong; let the vile person continue to be vile; let the one who does right continue to do right, and let the holy person continue to be holy" (Revelation 22:10–11). Now, what is that final precept if not a prescription for instituting maximal moral space, with every man set at liberty such that his or her freedom to choose between right and wrong is limited only by the requirement that every other man enjoy the same freedom? The final precept ties directly to James' prophecy: "you will be judged by the law that sets you free" (James 2:12).

What the final precept proclaims is, in effect, that for Providence to be fulfilled, liberty must be instituted, and that that requires right-doers not being allowed to force wrongdoers to do right, and, wrongdoers not being allowed to do any wrong that would prevent others from doing right. *That right there is a concise formula for liberty!*

And so, in summary, the New Testament teaches the ethos needed to be fit for liberty, namely: good-willed reasoning. The Good Book then concludes by codifying and mandating liberty, which it calls "the perfect law" (James 1:25).

Just as it took generations for universal emancipation to be realised after the Declaration of Independence was adopted, so it took centuries for the biblical precept formulating the concept of liberty to be grounded in a well-reasoned theory of rights, and for liberty to be enshrined in the lawbooks of an enlightened nation practicing agape.

"It was for freedom that Christ set us free."
Galatians 5:1

"Do not become slaves of people."
1 Corinthians 7:23

"[Agape] fulfils the law"
Romans 13:8

We can now understand what the author of the Declaration of Independence, Thomas Jefferson, was referring to when he wrote about the United States of America having "firm reliance on the protection of divine Providence," and why there is a Providential image and motto on the United States' Great Seal. It is no accident that the two original designs for the Great Seal by Founding Fathers – those of Benjamin Franklin and Thomas Jefferson – were both of biblical scenes.

Fast-forward to today, and the standard-bearing nation for rights has overshot the mark, and is now undermining the very liberty its patriots shed so much blood to institute. That overshooting and undermining has come about because America has shifted from previously having had a predominant ethos of agape, to today having a predominant ethos of philos toward some and ill-will toward others. The shift to philos toward some and ill-will toward others, rather than agape toward all, is epitomized in the U.S. government's counterfeiting of rights, sanctioned by voters, whereby ever more privileges are being classed and claimed as "rights" (see next chapter). This state of affairs has come about because too many Americans – as elsewhere in the world - are wanting the unearned, and are sanctioning themselves and others as being able to claim the unearned by "right." One could not dream up a more un-American notion!

Scripture warns what happens when agape stops being the ethos of a nation set at liberty: "For you, brothers, were called to freedom; [...] But if you bite and devour one another, take care that you are not consumed by one another" (Galatians 5:13–15). With American taxpayers owing themselves and others more than $120 trillion in unfunded liabilities for various privileges, or roughly one million dollars of unearned benefits per taxpayer (!)[11], the Great Nation is serving up its posterity on a platter to the current generation of ravenous consumers.

Rights can be righted again, and must be righted lest everything be lost, but it is going to take a moral revolution to do it: a revolution of men once again practicing agape, with the best of them working assiduously to remove privilege in all its forms.

The idea that rights can only be gained and liberty can only be attained by reason, is implied in Thomas Jefferson's wording of Declaration of Independence. Jefferson carefully chose his words when he inserted in the United States' founding document that, "We hold these truths to be self-evident, that all men are created equal, that they are endowed by their Creator with certain unalienable Rights." All men *are* created equal: each and every man is endued with reason; *not* to be endued with reason is not to be a man.

Jefferson explained what he meant by man's endowing "Creator" in a letter to John Adams dated 11 April 1823: "[Jesus'] doctrine of the Cosmogony of the world is very clearly laid down in the 3 first verses of the 1st. chapter of John … Which truly translated means 'in the beginning God existed, and reason (or mind) was with God, and that mind was God. This was in the beginning with God. All things were created by it, and without it was made not one thing which was made'. Yet this text, so plainly declaring the doctrine of Jesus that the world was created by the supreme, intelligent being, has been perverted by modern Christians to build up a second person of their tritheism by a mistranslation of the word {logos}. One of its legitimate meanings indeed is 'a word.' But, in that sense, it makes an unmeaning jargon: while the other meaning 'reason,' equally legitimate, explains rationally the eternal pre-existence of God, and his creation of the world."

And so, for Jefferson, reason – the faculty that makes a man a man, and in the image of God - is synonymous with the power of his or her Creator, that is, with the supreme Power creating all things and endowing man with rights. Consistent with this radical interpretation, the apostle John uses the word *logos* (λόγος or reason) to denote the Creator of all things (John 1:1).

The idea is also implied in the writings of John Locke. Locke wrote in his *Two Treatises of Government* (Book 2, paragraph 6) that, "The state of nature has a law of nature to govern it, which obliges everyone; *and reason, which is that law,* teaches all mankind, who will but consult it, that, being equal and independent, no one ought to harm another in his life, health, liberty or possessions" (emphasis added).

In the final paragraph of *A Summary View of the Rights of British America* (1774), Jefferson wrote in the spirit of Locke, "A free people [claim] their rights, as derived from the laws of nature, and not as the gift of their chief magistrate."

The implication of the above two passages when they are read together is that a free people claim their rights as being derived from reason, which is both their Creator (i.e., what makes them men) and the law of nature.

And there you have it. Rights and liberty were, are, and will always be anchored in reason, and can only ever be gained by reason – and specifically, by good-willed reasoning.

RIGHTS INSTITUTE

PHILOS vs AGAPE

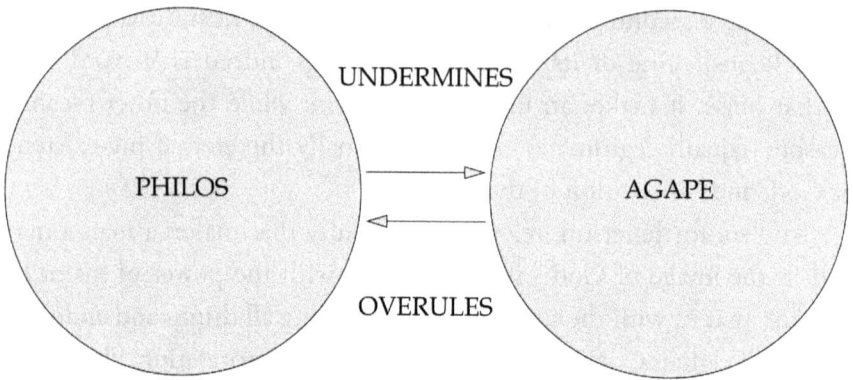

4. RIGHTS VERSUS PRIVILEGES

"A people that values its privileges above its principles soon loses both."
President Dwight D. Eisenhower, First Inaugural Address,
20 January 1953

A shortcut for grasping rights is to contrast them with privileges. Much of what is passed-off as rights today are not rights at all, but privileges.

Privilege originally meant "private law" (from Latin *privus* "one's own, private" and *lege* "law"). Privilege is any violation of rights that benefits and/or gives license to legally protected persons. In a legal context, privileges are diametrically opposed to rights because they empower and/or enrich the privileged at the expense of the unprivileged. Privileges always incur a cost, and that cost is always borne by the person whose rights are being violated. Rights, by comparison, are universal in nature and protect the moral space of all who do not violate them, while being denied equally to all who would, at no one's expense.

Whereas instituting rights results in liberty, which is freedom for all at the expense of none, instituting privileges results in license for some at the expense of others.

Economic privileges are entitlements given to certain persons at the expense of others, and include such things as government loans, bailouts, a mandated minimum wage, public housing, "free" healthcare and education, as well as such things as bank and taxi licenses, to name a few. They are the legal mechanism through which some people live at the expense of other people.

Privilege originated with monarchs bestowing entitlements on chosen subjects whilst claiming royal prerogative for themselves, all at the expense of others. Today, kings and queens have been replaced by a tyranny of welfare-peddling politicians and bureaucrats. Privileges are now being granted to members of a net consumptive class (i.e. to those who consume more than they produce) in the form of licenses, competition-stifling regulations, subsidies, public services, welfare payments and the like, all at the expense of members of the net productive class (i.e. those who produce more than they consume). The net consumptive class are our modern-day masters by proxy, while the net productive class are their serfs in all but name.

Think how poetic it is that the entity most responsible for empowering and encouraging the net consumptive class and its feeding frenzy is called the Fed (the Federal Reserve Bank). The Fed is an institution that enjoys a legal monopoly on the creation and control of money, or more accurately, on the creation and control of money substitutes. If that's not privilege, what is?

The closer one's economic proximity to the Fed, the more privileged one is. The entities closest to the Fed are government and commercial banks. This includes civil servants and employees of state-owned enterprises, but also private shareholders and employees of politically-connected corporations who benefit from artificially favorable loan terms (the ultimate perversion being negative interest rates), and in times of crisis, bailouts, both of which are supplied at the expense of net producers.

As Ayn Rand wrote in her 1963 essay *Man's Rights*: "If some men are entitled by right to the products of the work of others, it means that those others are deprived of rights and condemned to slave labor. Any alleged 'right' of one man, which necessitates the violation of the rights of another, is not and cannot be a right. No man can have a right to impose an unchosen obligation, an unrewarded duty or an involuntary servitude on another man. There can be no such thing as 'the right to enslave.'"[12]

That today's slaves enjoy modern conveniences, have more leisure time than their forebears, and in many cases, are wealthier than their masters (although this is fast changing), does not alter the role they are playing or the direction they are being led.

Another way to understand the difference between rights and privileges is to recognize how they are both legal claims on dues. Whereas rights are a claim on a single legitimate due, which is a negative one – not to be interfered with – privileges are claims on a multitude of concocted dues, all of which are positive – that others supply special benefits to the privileged, compelled by government force. (Note: the rights referred to here are fundamental rights, not contractual rights or the right of children to parental support, both of which involve moral obligations that are freely entered into by the contracting or parenting parties.)

More specifically, rights are reciprocal claims on the single obligation individuals owe one another under liberty: hands off me and what is rightfully mine. Privileges on the other hand are non-reciprocal claims on the lives and livelihoods of others under a legal system of permissions, regulations, bans, and subsidies, all of which have the aim of forcefully redistributing private property and controlling people's behavior, which in turn denies men their autonomy, moral space, rights, and equality before the law.

The negative due that are rights is claimed reciprocally through private property. The positive dues that are privileges are claimed exceptionally through private laws – laws that are particular to persons according to the group(s) they belong to, and in more corrupt societies, according to their proximity to political power, favors, bribery, and blackmail.

In the context of law, whereas privilege is any claim that involves a violation of rights, a right is any claim that negates privilege. Rights negate privilege by defining and sanctioning the moral space of individual men such that privilege-seekers are prevented from claiming what is not theirs by right. This makes rights and privileges mutually exclusive opposites.

Ayn Rand summed up the phenomenon of privileges masquerading as rights as follows: "A collectivist tyranny dare not enslave a country by an outright confiscation of its values, material or moral. It has to be done by a process of internal corruption. Just as in the material realm the plundering of a country's wealth is accomplished by inflating the currency – so today one may witness the process of inflation being applied to the realm of rights. The process entails such growth of newly promulgated 'rights' that people do not notice the fact that the meaning of the concept is being reversed. Just as bad money drives out good money, so these 'printing-press rights' negate authentic rights."[12]

At its root, politics is the struggle between those who want authentic rights to be the order of the day, and those who want privileges or "printing-press rights" to be the order – between those who seek to survive and prosper under liberty, and those who seek to survive and prosper under a system of coercions. When privileges usurp rights, with the shield of rights being replaced by the weapon of privilege, the struggle for moral space devolves into a fight among privilege-seekers over whose immoral space is going to win the day, and damn the consequences. Such is the direction that the world is heading in today … may it be righted!

RIGHTS vs PRIVILEGES

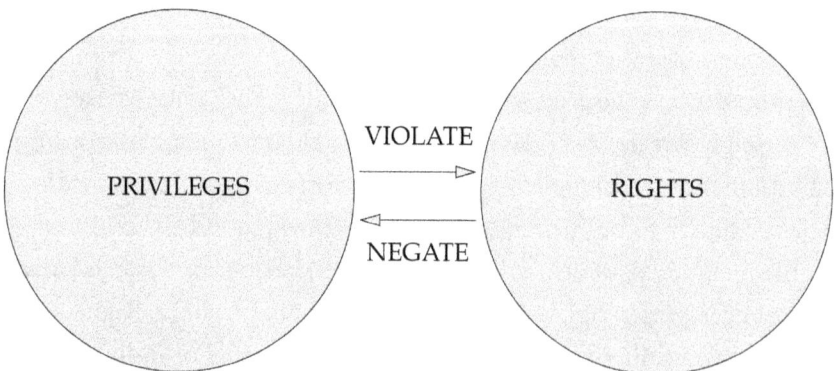

PRIVILEGES   VIOLATE →
                    ← NEGATE   RIGHTS

5. NATURE AND EPISTEMOLOGY OF RIGHTS

"Liberty lies in the hearts of men and women;
when it dies there, no constitution, no law, no court can save it;
no constitution, no law, no court can even do much to help it."
Learned Hand, "The Spirit of Liberty" speech,
21 May 1944

Now that you have grasped the essence of man, the concept of moral space, the ethos required for liberty to work, and the difference between rights and privileges, let's look more deeply at rights themselves.

An expanded definition of rights is as follows:

Rights are moral principles that compossibly define and sanction a man's freedom of action in a social context such that every man's moral space is maximized mutualistically.

This definition tells us what rights are when realized, namely: (a) principles, which means they are fundamental truths, which means they are discoverable, and once discovered, absolute; (b) moral, which means they serve as a guide to proper human action; (c) social, which means they pertain exclusively to interactions between individuals; (d) what defines and sanctions a man's freedom of action such that every man's moral space is maximized mutualistically, which means that rights are moral claims to freedom of action, and the capable-of-reasoning individual, not any group or collective, is the principal beneficiary of rights; and (e) compossible, which means that for a right to be a right, it must be consistent with every other right, and compatible with the conditions of existence required by man's nature for his or her proper survival.[13]

Dovetailing with this expanded definition of rights are the four stages of liberty realization, and the five stages of rights realization (see diagrams below).

The four stages of liberty realization begin with agape as the prevailing ethos, which in turn leads to men discovering and adopting rights. Rights define and maximize moral space, which in turn sets individual members of a society at liberty, with every man's autonomy protected in law.

STAGES OF LIBERTY REALIZATION | STAGES OF RIGHTS REALIZATION

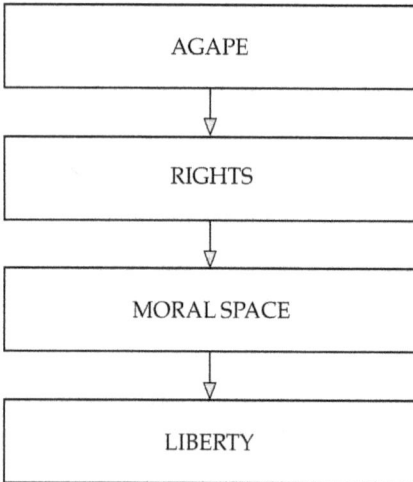

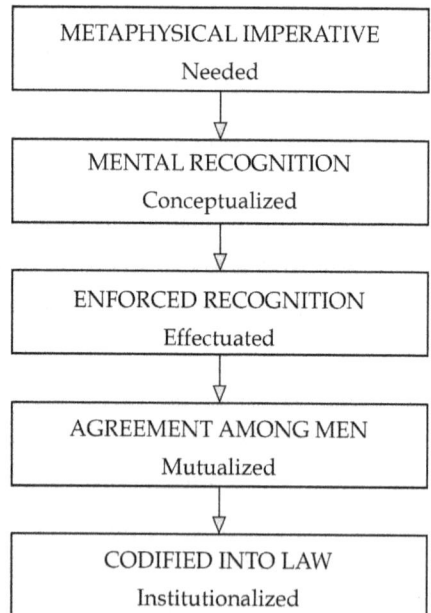

STAGES OF LIBERTY REALIZATION	STAGES OF RIGHTS REALIZATION
AGAPE	METAPHYSICAL IMPERATIVE Needed
RIGHTS	MENTAL RECOGNITION Conceptualized
MORAL SPACE	ENFORCED RECOGNITION Effectuated
LIBERTY	AGREEMENT AMONG MEN Mutualized
	CODIFIED INTO LAW Institutionalized

The five stages of rights realization deals with the various senses of "have" in the claim "I/you/we have rights," and is not to be confused with the process of conceptualizing "rights," which is the second of the five stages and is given below.

The first and fundamental stage of realizing rights is pre-realization, when rights are nothing more than a metaphysical imperative. It is in realizing that rights are a metaphysical imperative together with choosing to live as a man that rights become a moral imperative. The metaphysical imperative is this: if a man is to live as a man in society, he or she needs ample moral space. Only when that reality is understood, and moral principles are formulated to meet the need, do rights advance from being necessary conditions of existence required by man's nature for his or her proper survival (stage one), to being moral principles defining and sanctioning a man's freedom of action in a social context such that every man's moral space is maximized mutualistically (stage two). With the first stage, rights are *needed*.

In the second stage, rights are had in mind. Rights are had in mind when moral principles are formulated to satisfy the need in the first stage. In this second stage, rights are *conceptualized*; they are had as moral principles – moral principles that satisfy the conditions of existence required by man for his or her survival in society.

In the third stage, rights become effectual. With this stage, overwhelming retaliatory force is threatened against anyone who would violate rights, that is, against anyone who would intrude on another man's moral space. Rights having the backing of overwhelming retaliatory force are *effectuated*. It is possible for rights to be effectuated without an agreement existing among men, as in the case of a lone rational man successfully upholding his or her rights against irrational men. Without rights being effectuated, might is able to overpower right.

In the fourth stage, rights advance to being an agreement among rational men. With this stage, two or more enlightened men reach an agreement about what rights are, and unite to uphold them. With stage four, rights become *mutualized* moral principles. Mutualizing moral

23

principles forms a relationship between men. Again, the third and fourth stages do not necessarily actualize in that order.

It should be noted here that privileges result from irrational men skipping steps one and two, conceptualizing and/or reaching an agreement on wrongly conceived "rights," and effectuating those.

The fifth and final stage of realizing rights is when rights become an institution. This final stage, which perfects rights, is achieved when the conditions of existence required by man's nature for his or her proper survival are not only conceptualized as moral principles, effectuated and mutualized, they are also codified in law. With the fifth stage, rights progress to being *institutionalized*; they are had as an institution. Privileges can be institutionalized too, and often are, in violation of rights.

The above sets out the logical progression of realizing rights, from being conditions of existence required by man's nature for his or her proper survival (namely, having ample moral space), to being a conceptual recognition of and respect for that fact, to rights having effect by being backed by overwhelming retaliatory force threatened against all would-be rights violators, to being an agreement among enlightened men, to being an institution. Such is the development of rights from being a fact of reality, to being objective law; from being had as a metaphysical imperative, to being a moral imperative and had as an institution that does not sanction injustice.

Looked at another way, rights begin as something needed because of man's identity (stage one). They then progress to being had in mind as a result of men becoming enlightened about the truth of rights (stage two). Rights are only enjoyed though when they are upheld by lone defenders of rights, or by a group of defenders of rights, or, ideally, by institutions and law (stages three, four, and five, respectively).

It is important to note here that rights only concern the moral needs of man, not the material needs of humans. It is only when the moral needs of men are satisfied that the material needs of humans can be satisfied on a sustainable basis. History testifies to this. Unreasonable or not-yet-reasoning humans will always be dependent on reasoning men for their survival.

Identifying rights as being attached to a genome, or generated by legislators, or originating in a written document, or resulting from a majority vote, or being divorced from their social context, or separated from the rational mind that conceives them, are all flawed ways of arriving at rights. If and when it is adopted, a flawed concept of rights puts everyone's enjoyment of rights in jeopardy.

Identifying rights as being objectively identifiable moral principles that safeguard and preserve the identity of man in a social context by maximizing and mutualizing the moral space of all men, is the proper conception of rights.

Let us now hone in on and consider the critical distinctions between needing rights, having rights in mind, and enjoying rights.

To help you with what comes next, consider the flowchart below which lays out a proper epistemology for the various stages of realizing rights, that is, for grasping the meaning of "have" in the claim "I/you/we have rights" (again, not to be confused with the epistemology for conceptualizing rights themselves, which is given below):

EPISTEMOLOGY OF RIGHTS AS MORAL PRINCIPLES - STAGES OF REALIZATION

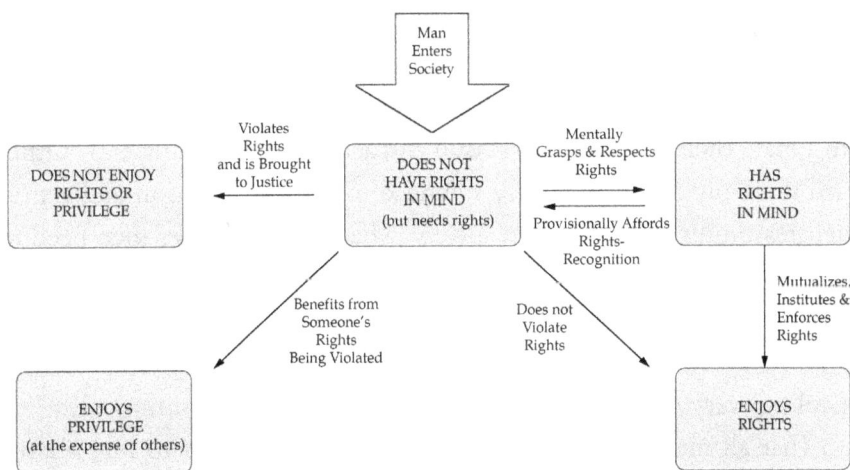

Once rights are conceived, they are no longer just a metaphysical imperative, they become a mental entity too (rights do not exist as an entity in any other respect).

The type of mental entity rights become is a moral principle, which is a type of concept, and is arrived at through a process of reasoning. This sense of having rights means having a moral code consistent with the conditions of existence required by man's nature for his or her proper survival in society. Conceptualized rights *are* that moral code – a code that defines and sanctions a man's freedom of action in a social context such that every man's moral space is maximized mutualistically.

When one makes the claim "I have rights," what one is really saying for that statement to mean anything is, "I have conditions of existence required by my nature as a man," and, "I have grasped and live by moral principles that maximize every man's moral space mutualistically, thereby satisfying the conditions of existence required by my and others' nature as men." Many people proclaim that they have rights when what they are really saying is "I am entitled to privileges," which means, "I want to be given something that is not mine by right." Such people haven't the foggiest idea about rights, and constitute today's privilege-seekers.

Let us turn now to how rights are conceptualized (i.e., stage 2 of the realization of rights).

In order to arrive at the concept "rights" objectively, one must make certain observations about reality, and apply logic to the observed facts. The chain of reasoning about the observed facts should be as follows: 1) "I am a man, therefore I need to reason and act on my reasoning"; 2) "Other men share my identity, so they too need to be able to reason and act on their reasoning"; 3) "When in society, what do I and other men need to be able to reason and act on our reasoning?" Answer: "Rights, which are moral principles that define and sanction every man's freedom of action in a social context such that moral space is maximized mutualistically, enabling every man to reason and act on their reasoning unimpeded."

That all men have certain rights – namely, the right to life, liberty, and the pursuit of happiness – is, as the Founding Fathers recognized, self-evident. It is self-evident to anyone who engages in a modicum of introspection. Let me demonstrate. Ask yourself: do *you* need your life, and to be free to act in accordance with your own reasoning (liberty), and not to have the product of your efforts taken from you without your consent (property), in order to be able to live as a man in society? If your answer is "no," it means you are confused about what it means to be a man. Try visualizing yourself stripped of your property, emaciated, and holed up in a prison camp undergoing excruciating torture, all because you were overheard saying something the ruling regime did not like. Now try answering the question again. If your answer is "yes," then congratulations! You have just grasped what fundamental rights are – the right of every man to life, liberty, and property.

Just because you have grasped what fundamental rights are, does not mean that others have or will, or even that you can enjoy rights in the meantime – that requires enforcement, mutualization, and ideally institutionalization, which means, respectively: threatening overwhelming retaliatory force against any and all would-be violators, obtaining the agreement of others, and codifying the principles in law.

In contrast to needing rights (which all men in a society do), and having rights in mind (which not all men do), enjoying rights means that rights are effectuated for everyone whether they have rights in mind or not, so long as one does not violate or threaten to violate rights.

It is *right* for men who have rights in mind to afford the recognition of rights to every other man (and at minimum, the right to become a man to all potential men), so long as those others are not violating or threatening to violate anyone's rights, regardless whether they have grasped them or not. That is because it costs nothing to make the recognition, yet it strengthens the institution of rights by enabling prospective rights-holders to grow into rights and become free men.

The difference between rights-holders reciprocating rights-recognition, and affording rights-recognition to they who have not yet grasped rights, is the difference between paying a due that is owed, and paying it forward. Take a moment to reflect on how the recognition of your own rights was paid forward as you grew into and grasped rights, and what moral obligation that entails on your part towards others.

Recapping now: For rights to be enjoyed by all who would not violate them – for there to be liberty – rights first have to be had in mind, meaning mentally grasped, by some. It is to those some that everyone else owes their enjoyment of rights, unless, that is, a man is able to effectuate their rights without anyone's help. Rights-holders must reciprocate rights-recognition if they want their own rights to be respected by others, and ought to afford rights-recognition to everyone else who has neither violated nor is threatening to violate rights for the same reason. Affording rights-recognition to they who have neither grasped nor violated nor are threatening to violate rights strengthens the institution of rights by enabling prospective rights-holders to exercise their autonomy and grow into the stature of free men.

GENUS/DIFFERENTIA OF RIGHTS

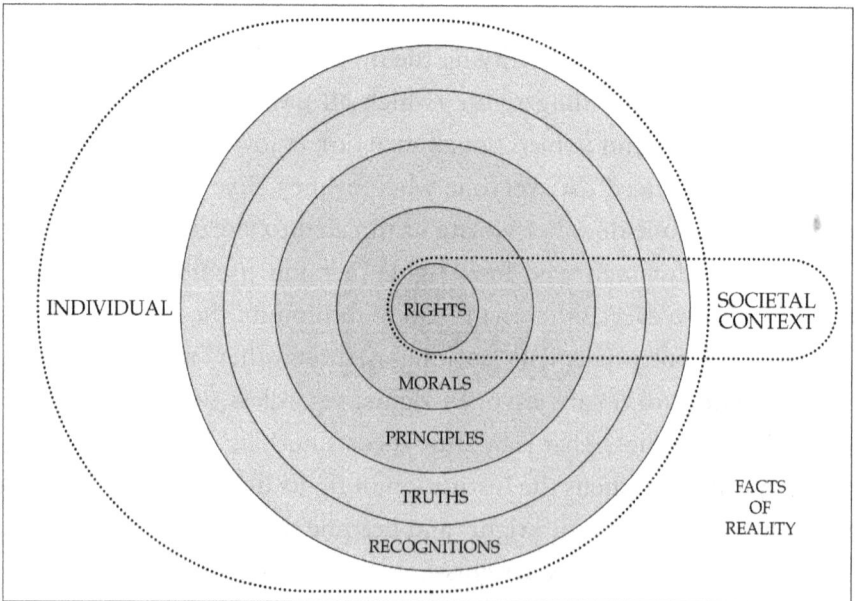

6. RIGHTS-RECOGNITION

*"Rightful liberty is unobstructed action according to our will
within limits drawn around us by the equal rights of others.
I do not add 'within the limits of the law' because law is often
but the tyrant's will, and always so when it violates
the rights of the individual."*

**Thomas Jefferson, letter to Isaac H. Tiffany,
4 April 1819**

Rights-recognition is the judicious application of rights. It is a negative due paid by those who have grasped and respect rights to others who have grasped and respect rights, and where affordable, is paid forward to prospective rights-holders in the hope and expectation that they will grow into and grasp and respect rights. The "due" paid and paid forward is this: not to violate rights, which means, not to initiate force against any person or their property, which means, not to intrude on anyone's moral space.

Rights-recognition should never be afforded to unreformed rights-violators, as that would be an injustice and put the effectuality of rights in jeopardy. Unreformed rights-violators pose a threat to rights. The principle to adhere to is this (per Rand): never grant the terms of reason to those who profess that they are going to deprive you of your reason.[14] The only just way to deal with initiations of force and threats to initiate force is to counter with overwhelming retaliatory force such that rights are secured. Performing that task is the only legitimate function of government, and the only path to justice, a peaceful society, and to men being able to live as men among men and not-yet men.

The affordability of paying rights-recognition forward to would-be rights violators, such as those who actively seek privilege and/or the abolition of the institution of rights, is a matter for rights-holders to decide as a nation. Although everyone has the right to investigate ideas and speak their mind without censorship, no one has a right to actually threaten rights, including conspiring to overturn or undermine the institution of rights. Right-holders must decide what they are willing to tolerate when rights-deniers band together and agitate with the aim of undermining, violating and/or doing away with the recognition of rights by political or revolutionary means.

The Founding Fathers were in full possession of their rights when they signed the Declaration of Independence, hence why it is written, "We *hold* these truths to be self-evident" (emphasis added). What is not well understood is that the Declaration of Independence paid forward a recognition of rights to every peaceful person on the planet. That recognition did not extend to rights-violators and would-be rights violators though, hence the line: "We … hold the rest of mankind, Enemies in War." The rest of mankind being enemies in war refers to those who are the enemies of rights – rights that the states of the Union united and the North later fought the South to uphold.

The Founding Fathers performed their magnanimous feat in the hope and expectation that all human beings might one day grow into the stature of free men and grasp and respect, mutualize and give effect to, and ultimately institutionalize rights. In so doing, Washington, Jefferson, Franklin, Madison, Adams, Hamilton et al. were the first and only legislators in history to found a nation on the principle of rights and set it on a course for liberty. I invite you to reflect on what an incredible achievement that was, and on how far the United States has veered from its chartered course today.

7. THE FUNDAMENTAL RIGHT, INDIVIDUALISM, AND CAPITALISM

"At the heart of that western freedom and democracy is the belief that the individual man, the child of God, is the touchstone of value, and all society, groups, the state, exist for his benefit. Therefore the enlargement of liberty for individual human beings must be the supreme goal and the abiding practice of any western society."
Robert F. Kennedy,
"Day of Affirmation" Speech (1963)

Although all men are created equal, not all rights are equal. The fundamental right, the one that all other rights owe their existence to, is the right to life, and more specifically, the right of every man to live *as* men, and for themselves. This idea is denoted by the term "individualism." Individualism, which holds that no man has a right to interfere in another man's life, is diametrically opposed to collectivism, which is the idea that a man's life is owned by and exists to serve the collective, the tribe, the mob, or else its agent, the rogue state.

There is nothing wrong with people banding together and forming a community to achieve a common goal, but when the goal involves violating individual rights, that is what is denoted by the term "collectivism."

When collectivism, or living for the group, tribe, mob, or rogue state, is the end sought, the means is invariably some form of socialism.

The regimes and legacies of socialism's greatest champions and practitioners - Hitler, Stalin, and Mao - are examples of what illegitimate (i.e. rights-violating) collectives lead to when they are allowed to reach their logical end, namely: institutionalized enslavement, starvation, poverty, death, war, even genocide, all the while enriching a political elite.

It must never be forgotten that the word "Nazi" is short for National *Socialism*, and that USSR is an initialism for Union of Soviet *Socialist* Republics. The empirical evidence of socialism's failure as a politico-economic system is the persistently poor and declining living standards of the USSR and Nazi Germany, both of which relied heavily on the alms or loot of other countries to prop themselves up. It was then showcased in the juxtaposing of East and West Germany, and again in the juxtaposing of North and South Korea. Venezuela is the latest example of the sort of outcome one can expect from socialism. To advocate for socialism today, after witnessing the proof of its failure to provide for man's well-being, after seeing its rabid antagonism towards man's nature as a moral agent, and after realizing its potency at producing poverty, slavery, death, destruction, and war, is to be a guilty party in all of the harm and misery it causes, and will cause, both now and in the future.

There can be no mistaking the incompatibility of collectivism and socialism, and individualism. Hitler himself said in a speech delivered at the Reichstag on 30 January 1937: "The main plank in the National Socialist program is to abolish the liberalistic concept of the individual." Mao proclaimed in his 1942 speech titled "Rectify the Party's Style of Work," that "We must combat individualism and sectarianism to enable our whole Party to march in step and fight for one common goal." According to legend, Joseph Stalin's "indispensable mentor," Vladimir Lenin, told Ivan Pavlov in an October 1919 meeting, "We must abolish individualism." Karl Marx, author of the Communist Manifesto, wrote in his essay "On the Jewish Question," that "human essence is the true collectivity of man."

Any political system that is anti-individualism and pro-collectivism is by that very fact at war with rights and with man. The truth is that man's essence is the true individuality of humanity.

The essence of socialism is its denial of man as a sovereign individual, of individual rights, and of property rights most of all. Under socialism, the means of production is invariably owned and/or controlled by the state, the proxy of "The People." Socialism's welfare statism has nothing to do with charity though. By definition, charity is voluntary giving. Socialism's "giving" is the forced redistribution of private property, meaning, the state's distribution of plundered wealth.

It is interesting to note that socialism is an ancient idea that first came to the West as an outlandish fiction. In his play *Ecclesiazusae* ("Assembly-women") written in 391 B.C., Aristophanes parodies what can only be described as socialism, albeit with a feminist bent. The plot of the play involves Athenian women seizing control of government and banning all private property. Praxagora, the lead character whose name means "act of The People's assembly," describes the coup as follows: "I shall begin by making land, money, everything that is private property, common to all." Praxagora also demands equal pay for everyone and a unified standard of living, as well as parental responsibilities being shared by the community. Once Praxagora's socialism is enacted, a character called "The Selfish Man" resists and protests, calling his neighbor a fool for giving up their property to support the crazy new order of things. A lavish "feast" then ensues, a metaphor for the consumptive nature of socialism.

The twentieth century saw Aristophanes' outlandish fiction become reality, less the feminism, in Nazi (and later East) Germany, the USSR, China, North Korea, Vietnam, Cuba, Laos, Afghanistan, Albania, Angola, Benin, Bulgaria, Congo, Czechoslovakia, Ethiopia, Grenada, Hungary, Kampuchea, Mongolia, Mozambique, Poland, Romania, Somalia, Tuva, Yemen, and Yugoslavia, all to disastrous effect. Sir Winston Churchill summed up socialism as follows: "Socialism is the philosophy of failure, the creed of ignorance, and the gospel of envy … The inherent virtue of Socialism is the equal sharing of miseries."[15]

When individualism, or living for oneself at no one else's expense, is the ends, the means is always going to be capitalism. Capitalism is the politico-economic system that recognizes individual rights. Capitalism upholds the principle that each and every individual should be free to live for themselves, so long as they do not interfere with the right of other individuals to do the same. "Live and let live" is capitalism's catch-cry, with the means of production held in private hands, and free market forces peacefully guiding those means into the ablest hands to manage. Capitalism makes it possible to become wealthy by serving rather than plundering or enslaving one's fellow man.

Capitalism is not an experiment; it is the proven system – a system designed for man according to man's nature. It is not perfect, but it is the best we have, and can ever have. It is socialism in its various guises that has been the experiment, and that experiment has failed abysmally. By forbidding force and fraud from social interactions, capitalism has consistently demonstrated that it leads men towards freedom and prosperity through reason and persuasion, rather than towards slavery and poverty through force and fear, as socialism does. Capitalism gives men the means and freedom to be charitable, while at the same time reducing the number of people needing charity. Sir Winston Churchill summed up capitalism as follows: "The inherent vice of capitalism is the unequal sharing of blessings."[15]

It is only in the last quarter century or so that we have all been able to communicate anything, anywhere, instantly, virtually for free. A vast resource of knowledge is now at our fingertips, essentially for free. We can listen to our favorite musicians, view our favorite artists, and read our favorite authors on demand, for next to nothing. Travel is faster and safer than ever before. Food is more plentiful than ever before. Life expectancy is longer than ever before. Child mortality is lower than it has ever been. Literacy is higher than it has ever been. Healthcare is better than it has ever been. Democracy is more prolific than it has ever been. Extreme poverty has all but been eradicated, with poverty only a relative measure now. All of these things are the blessings of capitalism, not socialism.

It is capitalism that broke the chains of slavery in the nineteenth century. It is capitalism that emancipated women and people of color in the twentieth century. Moreover, it is capitalism that has caused the unprecedented rise in living standards we are still precariously enjoying today – precariously because lately socialism has been making inroads into the United States of America, the bastion of capitalism. Those inroads include the adoption of a central banking system and an irredeemable debt-based monetary system designed to help government borrow beyond its means, artificial and easy monetary policies, historically high levels of peacetime taxation, a plethora of government welfare programs that give voters free stuff in exchange for giving up their freedom, and many aspects of life and business that now require a bureaucrat's permission just to be conducted legally. *All of these things are socialist, not capitalist, measures.* America today is no longer capitalist. Today's America is a mixed-economy, meaning a mixture of freedoms and controls.

What is most concerning is that socialists and socialism's sympathizers are succeeding at convincing an ever larger portion of the population that capitalism is to the blame for the problems caused by the socialist elements that have been introduced into Western economies. How to upend capitalism? Establish a system *in the name of* capitalism that destroys capital by stealth, then blame capitalism for the inevitable economic collapse. This is what is happening today, with Fabian socialists now on the verge of a victory they have fought so long and hard to win, but it is victory that will spell defeat for everyone in the end if it is allowed to happen.

In the order of things, capitalism comes first, with socialism following in capitalism's absence. This ordering is reflected in the word capitalism coming from the Latin word *caput*, meaning "head"; capitalism is the head economic system that requires people to use their heads. The word socialism derives from the Latin word *sequor*, meaning "to join to and follow," as socialism does capitalism. Socialism joins to, follows, and ultimately infects and destroys capitalism, as a deadly parasite does its host if not rooted out. Capitalism is first. Socialism is last. Capitalism is the highest. Socialism is the lowest. Capitalism rewards leaders. Socialism rewards followers. Capitalism brings life. Socialism brings death. Even Karl Marx recognized that socialism follows capitalism as a matter of course, but he wrongly concluded it was as a progression and not a regression.

Capitalism is the politico-economic system that is fueled by agape. Socialism is the politico-economic system that is fueled by philos at best, and ill-will at worst.

Those who are driven by envy, power-lust, and wanting the unearned aside, socialists tend to have good intentions. But as the ancient proverb rightly observes: the road to hell is paved with good intentions. Good intentions alone are never enough to produce good outcomes. Producing good outcomes requires agape, with goodwill being guided by reason, and not by feelings, wants and wishes, as with philos.

Today's global push to adopt socialist measures to combat environmental problems, and the phenomenon of climate change in particular, is a case in point. All that needs to be said about the latter is what former Libertarianz leader Bernard Darnton once did: "We know that socialism is immoral and unworkable at seventeen degrees. What makes anyone think it'll be different at nineteen degrees?"[16]

People are supporting socialist measures to combat a changing climate because they *feel* it is the right thing to do, not because it actually is. Planting lots of trees and adopting nuclear power is really all that needs to be done to offset any excess gas-of-life (i.e., CO_2) emissions, but you will not find hardened socialists espousing these two solutions as a be-all and end-all, because neither hand totalitarian power over to them, and it would allow capitalists to continue capitalizing, which is their real bugbear.

Capitalism is the system of voluntary cooperation, fueled by agape, that upholds individual rights. Socialism is the system of forced impositions, fuelled by philos (and/or envy), that counterfeits and violates rights. Only a system of voluntary cooperation fueled by agape, with property rights and nuisance torts as legal protections, has a chance of solving the world's social and environmental problems in tandem. The simple fact is that if agape is missing, no system can produce good outcomes in the long run.

When rights are formulated to recognize the most fundamental right - the right of every man to live his or her own life for him or herself – the smallest political 'minority' on earth, individual man, is then made the principal beneficiary of rights. If enough individuals unite to uphold the sanctity of rights, *individuals united* can then become the largest political majority on earth as well. That exciting possibility poses a genuine threat to privilege-seekers and collectivists, which is why machinating politicians, bureaucrats, and welfare-pushers, who are the privilege-seekers' representatives and facilitators, go to such great lengths to cajole the voting public into thinking primarily in terms of what groups they belong to, such as by race, culture, religion, gender, sexual preference, age, nationality, ethnicity, relative level of wealth or income, etc., rather than in terms of their manhood and individuality. Power-peddlers and power-seekers bribe members of groups who will vote them into power by implicitly promising to violate the rights of individuals who will not. That is not and can never be right.

Identity politics is the timeless ploy of oppressors to divide and conquer individuals and do away with man's autonomy. Hence why political oppressors form *parties*. The word party comes from the verb to part, from Latin *partio*, which means "I divide." To institute and uphold rights and annul privilege, an enlightened people doesn't need a party or division, they need a unity: a union of and for individual men upholding rights. The result of such a union would bring about radical laissez-faire capitalism, the only political system that champions the Rights of Man – as it did, albeit imperfectly, after the United States of America was founded (imperfectly, because lawmakers did not apply the country's founding principles to all men consistently).

To understand why capitalism is the superior system, consider what Henry Hazlitt said in a speech to the Chamber of Commerce of the United States in Washington, DC, on April 30, 1962: "The superior freedom of the capitalist system, its superior justice, and its superior productivity are not three superiorities, but one. The justice follows from the

freedom, and the productivity follows from the freedom and the justice."
Amen to that.

To recap, the solution to the world's social and political problems, now and always, is for people to unite on the ethos of agape, which will in turn lead them to unite on the principle of individualism, and therewith to unite on the Rights of Man, which necessarily results in liberty when a maximization and mutualization of moral space is effectuated. Enlightened men naturally adopt capitalism as the means to that end because it is the only politico-economic system that is consistent with rights, liberty, and the nature of man.

SOCIALISM vs CAPITALISM

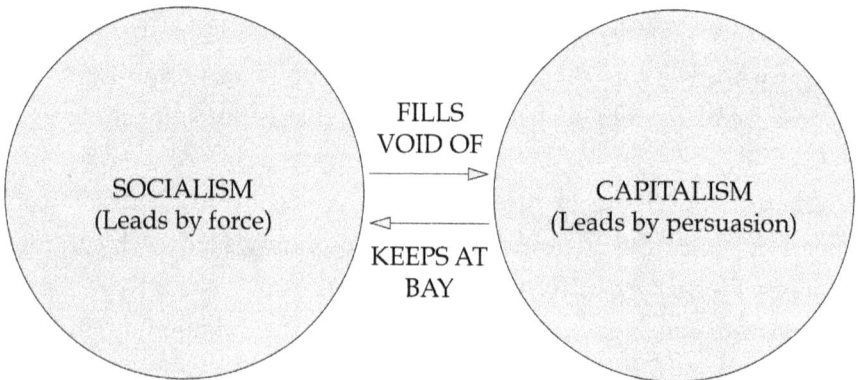

SOCIALISM
(Leads by force)

FILLS
VOID OF

KEEPS AT
BAY

CAPITALISM
(Leads by persuasion)

8. COMPOSSIBILITY

Compossibility is a philosophical concept of Gottfried Wilhelm Leibniz. It denotes non-contradiction among members and their properties. Compossible means able to exist with as a harmonious whole, a consistent composite.

Compossiblity is different to compatibility, which is the ability of one thing to coexist with another in a pairing. The common characteristic of compossibility and compatibility is consistency; with the former, everything is consistent with everything else, while with the latter, one thing is consistent with another.

For a set of alleged rights to be a legitimate set of rights, the set needs to be compatible with the conditions of existence required by man's nature for his or her survival, *and* every right in that set needs to be compossible with every other right, all with all. If an alleged right is incompossible with any of the other alleged rights in a set of alleged rights, it means that the set does not qualify as a legitimate set of rights. This is not to say that all of the alleged rights in an incompossible set are illegitimate, just that the set is not itself a legitimate one. Incompossibilty is a litmus test for whether a set of alleged rights is legitimate one or not. A set of alleged rights that is incompossible necessarily engenders privilege and violates rights.

History's most notable example of a set of compossible rights is the rights enumerated in the 1776 Declaration of Independence of the United States of America. They include the right to life, liberty, and the pursuit of happiness, and to alter or abolish and replace any form of government that becomes destructive of those ends. The last right is seldom quoted, but it is the right the Founding Fathers exercised when they declared independence from an oppressive British Crown. All four rights enumerated in the Declaration of Independence are compossible; each is consistent with, not contradictory of, the others, and all are compatible with the conditions of existence required by man's nature for his or her survival in society.

A fifth right was recognized in the US Constitution, ratified in 1787: the exclusive right of inventors and authors to reproduce their writings and discoveries for a limited time. In other words, the US Constitution gave legal effect to intellectual property rights. No other right is mentioned in US Constitution, only powers delegated. All other rights are implied in the founding five.

All of the rights listed in the original Bill of Rights – a document ratified in 1791 and known as the Ten Amendments – are compossible with and implied by those recognized in the Declaration of Independence and the Constitution when those three documents are read as one. Rights recognized by the Ten Amendments, all of which serve to limit the powers delegated to Congress under the Constitution, include but are not limited to (as stated in Amendments IX and X): freedom of religion, expression, and assembly (Amendment I), self-defense (Amendment II), privacy of property (Amendments III and IV), and swift justice (Amendments V, VI, VII, and VIII).

Critical to the legitimacy of the rights recognized in the three founding documents of the United States of America is that compossibility was maintained.

Failure to consistently practice the principles laid out in the founding documents aside, the first time incompossibility was introduced to the founding documents was with the addition of the Sixteenth Amendment in 1913 – the same year the Federal Reserve Bank came into existence – which empowered Congress to levy income taxes without taxpayers' consent (or so it has been interpreted). That Amendment was enacted despite the Supreme Court ruling in 1895 that the imposition of an income tax during peacetime is unconstitutional (*Pollock vs. Farmers' Loan Trust Company*). Shortly after the Sixteenth Amendment was ratified by Congress, the Eighteenth Amendment was ratified, prohibiting the manufacture and sale of alcohol. Neither the Sixteenth nor the Eighteenth Amendments are compossible with the rights listed in the Declaration of Independence, or with the original Ten Amendments to the Constitution. The Eighteenth Amendment was so starkly in violation of the Rights of Man that it was repealed in 1933.

The Sixteenth Amendment is still in effect today, and has become, together with the Federal Reserve Act and legal tender laws, the thin edge of the wedge that has opened the door to America's metamorphosis into a society of privilege-seekers. Prior to that door being opened, America had been an enlightened society of rights-instituters, evidenced in the gradual emancipation of all men consistent with the country's founding principles.

Thankfully, America's metamorphosis into a socialist state is not yet complete. If enough people of good-willed reasoning act to repeal the Sixteenth Amendment and abolish the Fed, its debt-based fiat money system, and legal tender laws, a set of compossible rights can still be instituted.

In contrast to the compossible set of rights upon which the United States was originally founded, a clear-cut example of incompossible "rights" is the United Nations' Universal Declaration of Human Rights, which was ratified in 1948. The Universal Declaration of Human Rights is a set of alleged rights, based on four so-called "freedoms" proclaimed by Franklin D. Roosevelt, the socialist-leaning US president whose government plundered the gold of US citizens in April of 1933. Those four "freedoms" are: freedom of speech, freedom of worship, freedom from want, and freedom from fear. The first two freedoms are legitimate rights. Freedom from want and fear however, which are meant to be taken literally, are not legitimate rights. Ask yourself: how can the productive members of a society be free from fear when the consumptive members are being promised the "right" to be free from want? Can a slave be free from fear if he is held responsible for his master being free from want? (These are rhetorical questions which serve to illustrate the concept of incompossibility.)

The Universal Declaration of Human Rights proclaims the so-called rights of "social security" (Article 22), "favourable remuneration" (Article 23), "rest and leisure" (Article 24), "food, clothing, housing and medical care" (Article 25), and "free education" (Article 26), together with the right "to own property alone as well as in association with others" and to not be "arbitrarily deprived of [one's] property" (both Article 17). What the first five so-called rights in that list ignore is that a right is and can only ever be the right to perform an action, and to suffer or enjoy the consequences free from interference by other men. This includes pursuing, creating, keeping, using, and disposing of one's property, or doing something to or with one's own body, as one sees fit, so long as one's actions do not violate the rights of others.

A right is never a claim that imposes an unchosen obligation on others to supply a value – *that is what a privilege is*. A legitimate right only ever imposes a negative obligation on others – not to interfere – which in turn means respecting the lives, liberty, and property of everyone who is beholden to rights.

One has the right to educate oneself and to pursue an education, to work and buy goods and services with the product of one's own effort. But as soon one claims entitlement to an education, a job, food, or clothing or the like, someone else then has to fund and/or provide those things at the point of a gun, that is, in response to the threat of government force. This in turn means that one has shifted from recognizing a right, to asserting and claiming privilege – to claiming the "right to enslave."

The set of privileges laid out in Articles 22, 23, 24, 25, and 26 (among others) of the Universal Declaration of Human Rights, needs to be paid and/or supplied by someone. Their inclusion sanctions the violation of legitimate rights specified elsewhere, such as those listed in Article 17, to pay for the program. Today, the provision of privileges stipulated in the UN's declaration is being facilitated by governments around the world through the enactment of taxation without consent (a form of extortion), artificially inflating the money supply (an insideous form of theft), and permission-based schemes involving licensing, all of which arbitrarily deprive individuals of their rightful property, or otherwise violate their rights.

The program and declaration of the United Nations assumes a collectivist premise, and is fundamentally socialist in nature.

Ironically, the final article of the Universal Declaration of Human Rights, Article 30, states that, "Nothing in this Declaration may be interpreted as implying for any State, group or person any right to engage in any activity or to perform any act aimed at the destruction of any of the rights and freedoms set forth herein." The inconvenient truth is that any set of alleged rights that is either incompossible or incompatible with man's nature, as the UN's set most certainly is, is self-invalidating and self-destructive. There is no such thing as a right to privilege!

9. PROPERTY RIGHTS:
THE IMPLEMENTARY RIGHT

*"When plunder becomes a way of life for a group of men in a society,
over the course of time they create for themselves a legal system that
authorises it and a moral code that glorifies it."*
Frédéric Bastiat,
Economic Sophisms, **2nd series (1848), Chapter 1**

Whereas the law of identity is source of all rights, and the right to life is the fundamental right, the right to property is the sole implementary right. It is only by recognizing and upholding the right to property that the right to life and liberty can be enjoyed. Or as Shakespeare put it: "You take my house, when you do take the prop that doth sustain my house; you take my life, when you do take the means whereby I live."[17]

Ayn Rand explained it best: "Without property rights, no other rights are possible. Since man has to sustain his life by his own effort, the man who has no right to the product of his effort has no means to sustain his life. The man who produces while others dispose of his product, is a slave. Bear in mind that the right to property is a right to action, like all the others: it is not the right to an object, but to the action and the consequences of producing or earning that object. It is not a guarantee that a man will earn any property, but only a guarantee that he will own it if he earns it. It is the right to gain, to keep, to use and to dispose of material values."[18]

And: "The right to agree with others is not a problem in any society; it is the right to disagree that is crucial. It is the institution of private property that protects and implements the right to disagree – and thus keeps the road open to man's most valuable attribute (valuable personally, socially, and objectively): the creative mind."[19]

In the quest to identify and uphold authentic rights, it is critical to understand what property is, that is because property must be discerned from plunder in the rights equation if rights are to be properly recognized and judiciously upheld. Just as when the concept "man" becomes confused, rights become confused, so when the concept "property" becomes confused, rights become confused. Confusion about who is the subject of rights (i.e., individual men or the human species as such) or about what constitutes property, necessarily causes privilege to creep in and take the place of rights.

The nature of property is found in the first instance in the various etymologies of the word in the classical sense of that science. Classical etymology recognizes that the true sense of certain words may be found in the words themselves, and differs from modern etymology, which is the study of the historical development of words.

The first etymology of property in the classical sense is *proper + -ty*. Property is that which is proper to the person owning it. It is obviously not proper for property to be owned by a thief, a blackmailer, or an extortionist. It is only proper for property to be owned by the individual whose industry brought it into existence, and to anyone who acquires it thereafter without the use of coercion, force or fraud. Thieves, blackmailers, and extortioners do not own property, they own *plunder*. Plunder and property are, like rights and privileges, mutually exclusive opposites. One person's plunder is always someone else's stolen property, just as one person's privilege is always someone else's violated right.

The first etymology is related to the second, which is the conventional one. Modern etymologists theorize that the word "property" derives from the Latin words *prōprius* and *prōprīvus*, both of which mean "one's own."

Prōprius joins the prefix *pro-* which means "befitting," with *prius* which means "first, original." Property is therefore that which befits its originator. The word *prōprīvus* is slightly different and joins *pro-* ("befitting") with *privus* ("private") to render the idea that property is that which befits privacy. And so it does; property befits its originator and his or her privacy.

Getting creative now, a third etymology is *prop + -e- + r(igh)t + -y.* Property props up rights, including the right to life, as Shakespeare poetically recognized it does. It is only through the institution of private property that rights can be instituted.

A fourth way to look at the word is *pro- + (o)per(a) + -ty*, denoting property befitting work. "Opera" means work in Latin. This last etymology brings to mind the wage-fund doctrine, which is the economic theory that recognizes that all wages, and by extension all paid work, is funded by savings or capital, meaning by property. When there is no property in the form of savings or capital, employers cannot pay their workers. Without property to fund workers' salaries, coercion is the only means of making a man work for his or her fellow man. Enter socialism.

So much to be learned in a word!

We shall now look at how property is created and expires.

The writer who first identified the true nature of property is an unappreciated nineteenth-century French economist by the name of Frédéric Bastiat.

In his main treatise on property, Bastiat wrote, "In our relations with one another, we are not owners of the utility of things, but of their value, and value is the appraisal made of reciprocal services."[20] Bastiat's breakthrough was identifying *value*, not things or their utility, as constituting property. Value is the property of whomever makes the causational effort to bring the value into existence and values it. This notion is expressed in the nineteenth-century idea that one has property *in* things, not that things are themselves property. Calling a thing property is metonymic (i.e. a substitutive but inaccurate use of a word).

Carl Menger, founder of the Austrian school of economics, advanced Bastiat's idea of value-based property by demonstrating that the marginal utility of goods is what quantifies value. Menger recognized that individuals appraise the value of things not as grand totalities, but on the margin, hence his term "marginal utility." For example, one's first unit of water is used to prevent oneself and one's loves ones from dying of thirst. One's second unit of water might be used for washing oneself. One's third unit might be used to water one's plants or wash one's car. One is willing to expend or exchange more of one's effort to obtain the first unit of water, and ever less for the second and subsequent units. With this example, one does not quantify the value of a unit of water by looking at water as a whole, but by determining the marginal utility of each unit of water, with the value in an exchange diminishing as the marginal utility of each unit of the good diminishes.

With his theories of marginal utility and the economics of scarcity, Menger proved that the value of labor in a free market is determined by an appraisal of the value of the marginal utility of goods and services produced by labor, *not* by appraising the labor directly, which is a Marxist error.

Half a century later, Ayn Rand observed that labor or effort is only the means of creating value, but is not a value itself. Value, she theorized, can only be arrived at by making good value judgments, which is why the creative valuing mind is the ultimate source of all property. This idea is illustrated in how if a caveman finds a sharp flint stone and begins cutting things with it, it is his mind that brings property to the stone. If a second caveman discovers that the same stone struck against another type of stone, say pyrite, causes a spark, and that he can start a fire that way, he has then brought another property to the stone. By trading a few fish for the stone, the second caveman secures his property right in both the flint and the pyrite for the purpose of starting fires. Note that nothing changed with the stone materially, and no physical effort was expended in creating the property; the property in each case is the value the caveman brought to the item using their ingenuity. Such is the nature of intellectual property rights and how property and its associated value expires, or should expire.

A litmus test for whether one has property *in* a thing is whether it can be shown that one's effort, and one's mental effort especially, has given rise to the value of the thing, and has done so without violating anyone's property rights in the process. If it is not possible to demonstrate this, and specifically, how the elements of nature have been rearranged or newly applied by one's effort to produce new value (and in the case of yet-to-be propertied land or resources, how the elements of nature will be rearranged or newly applied by one's effort to produce new value), then one has no claim to having created any property (or provisional property).

For example, if a person or a collective such as a tribe or a nation claims to have property in land or resources, the question must be asked: how did the person's or collective's efforts give rise to the value of the land or resources over and above what nature supplies gratis? In other words, how has the person's or collective's mental and/or physical efforts transformed the land or resources into something more valuable than it was previously? If the answer is that new value has been created because of what the person or the collective has built, farmed, or otherwise produced through their purposeful effort, then the claim to having property in the land or its resources is a legitimate one, even if the property is communally owned (people have a right to communalize if they wish, so long as they do so voluntarily and do not violate the rights of individuals in the process). But if the answer is that the person or the collective has merely had a custom of collecting, consuming, or otherwise exploiting what nature produces effortlessly, such as hunting its game, picking its wild fruits, cutting down its trees without replanting any, collecting water from streams, or foraging, then the claim to having property in the land or its resources is unfounded. It is unfounded because no value has been created in the land or its resources by the effort of the person or collective. Living off land or resources without farming, developing, or otherwise positively transforming them to satisfy human wants or needs does not create property in anything other than the individual items hunted, picked, collected, or foraged. A forager has property in the apple he or she picked from the wild, but not in the apple tree, and not even in the picked apple if someone else planted the tree. (One of the features of property is that new property may be acquired by accession, meaning that an apple on a planted tree is an accession of that tree – it is new value resulting from effort expended in planting the tree, and is the property of the one who planted the tree.)

When privileged individuals such as monarchs or tribal leaders claim sovereignty over land and resources untransformed for the better by their own efforts, what they are really claiming is *dominion*, not property. When the rest of us claim ownership of land and resources in which we have no property, what we are really claiming is *possession* or estate. Having dominion over or possession of a thing does not equate to having property in that thing.

In his treatise, Bastiat poignantly explains the distinction as follows: "Unfortunately, at the very beginning they made the error of confusing utility with value. They attributed inherent value, independent of any human service, to both raw materials and the forces of Nature. Once this error was made, the right to property could be neither understood nor justified."[21]

Bastiat further observed that there are two kinds of utility or satisfactions of wants: utility resulting from valuable effort (i.e. effort that results in property), which he called onerous utility, and utility that comes free of charge from "Providence," which he called gratuitous utility.

Gratuitous utility is the satisfaction of any want that does not involve expenditure of effort, either mental or physical. Utility that is supplied gratis by nature includes such things as the heat and light of the sun, clean air, pristine streams for drinking or bathing, rainwater, picturesque views of natural habitats, the land on which we traverse, and so on. Gratuitous utility also includes intellectual property that has expired and entered the public domain, that is, knowledge that is freely given to us which saves us the effort of making our own discoveries.

Bastiat's concept of communal wealth is not the socialist's idea of public property, which is really the dispossession of free or gratuitous utility, and the plundering of private property. Far from it. Bastiat's concept of communal wealth denotes the aggregate of nature's bounty together with any extinguished property, meaning, intellectual property that has entered the public domain (see diagram below).

Bastiat concluded that "the spirit of property, is continually to enlarge the communal domain," with private property being the "pioneer" of communal wealth, and the source of an ever-expanding pool of gratuitous utility, whereby ample communal wealth or gratuitous utility enables mankind to move ever closer to an effortless existence. Bastiat expressed the formula as follows:[22]

$$\text{Want} \left\{ \begin{array}{c} \textbf{Gratuitous Utility} \\ \textbf{Onerous Utility} \end{array} \right\} \text{Satisfaction}$$

The idea of an ever-expanding gratuitous utility resulting from property expiration is expressed in an observation by economist Thomas Sowell: "The cavemen had the same natural resources at their disposal as we have today, and the difference between their standard of living and ours is a difference between the knowledge they could bring to bear on those resources and the knowledge used today."[23]

Ownership of gratuitous utility alone is never a legitimate claim to property; it is properly speaking a claim to possession or dominion. Unlike property, which is proper to the person (or group) owning it because their effort and judgment created the value, possession means "having the power to sit on," from Latin *potis* "power/able to" and *sedeo* "I sit on, hold fast to." Having possession of a thing without also having property in it is just that: it is to sit on free utility and/or plunder.

The word dominion means "to lord over," from Latin *dominus*, "lord." The idea of possessing or lording over utility divorced from having property in it is an old-world concept which has caused most of history's wars. Warring parties would fight over who has the "right" (but really the privilege) to possess and/or lord over free utility and/or plundered property. In order for proprietorship to replace lordship and wrongful ownership, new value, meaning new onerous utility, meaning new property, needs to be created and given rightful ownership.

Rightful ownership on account of having property in what is owned, as against merely possessing or lording over what is owned, is a new-world concept that has led to unprecedented peace and prosperity, but has been tainted by the envy and greed of those who have either not been able or not been bothered to create property of their own. Proprietorship, not possession or dominion, is the enlightened approach to implementing rights.

MAKE UP OF PROPERTY

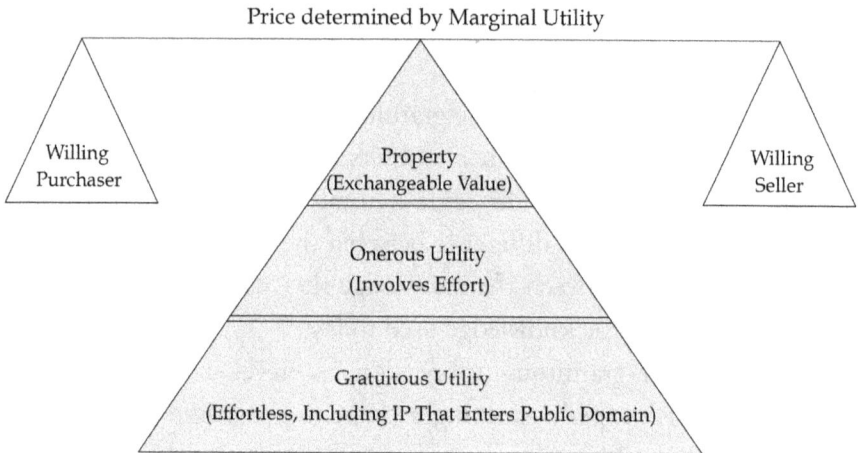

Price determined by Marginal Utility

Willing Purchaser

Property
(Exchangeable Value)

Onerous Utility
(Involves Effort)

Gratuitous Utility
(Effortless, Including IP That Enters Public Domain)

Willing Seller

Referring now to the Make Up of Property diagram,[24] onerous utility is any utility resulting from physical and/or intellectual effort that produces potentially exchangeable value, with the quantum of the value being determined by the marginal utility of what is being valued. It is from the exchangeability of value brought into existence by useful effort that property emerges. All onerous utility, and therefore property, employs gratuitous utility. For example, every painter employs the chemical properties supplied gratis by nature and discovered by the effort of other men before adding his or her own onerous utility to the mix to produce a tradable and therefore valuable painting.

Gratuitous utility is the aggregate of nature's freely available resources together with any intellectual property that has entered into the public domain.

In a capitalistic and therefore free society, onerous utility is constantly being replaced by gratuitous utility as obstacles preventing effortless living are removed because of the expiry of intellectual property, which results in freely available knowledge. In a socialistic society, the reverse happens: gratuitous utility is constantly being replaced by onerous utility as new obstacles are introduced in the form of regulations, licenses, taxes, and prohibitions, all of which introduce artificial costs and burdens, causing a depletion of gratuitous utility, and the creation of the phenomenon known as the Tragedy of the Commons.

Here is the process in Bastiat's own words:

"[God] placed men in the midst of these raw materials and these forces and bestowed them upon him gratis. To them men applied their energies; and in so doing they performed services for themselves. They also worked for one another; and in so doing they rendered reciprocal services. These services, when compared for purposes of exchange, gave rise to the idea of value, and value to the idea of property … But the forces and the raw materials, originally given gratis to man by God, remained, still are, and always will be, gratis, however much, in the course of human transactions, they may pass from hand to hand; for, in the appraisals that their exchange necessitates, it is *human services*, and not the *gifts of God*, that are *evaluated*. From this it follows that there is not one among us who, provided only our transactions be carried out in freedom, ever ceases to enjoy these gifts. A single condition is attached: we must ourselves perform the labor necessary to make them available to us, or, if someone else takes this trouble for us, we must pay him the equivalent in other pains that we take for him. If what I assert is true, then certainly the right to property is unassailable."[25]

By "labor" Bastiat means mental or physical labor.

In a division of labor society that has been set at liberty, where each man produces what others consume, and others produce what he consumes, every man becomes a proprietor in proportion to the appraised services he or she renders to his or her fellow man. For the man who has no valuable services to offer, he or she has just two alternatives to survive: to seek alms from those who do have valuable services to offer, or to plunder property. Socialists, being they who would forcefully take from one and give to another and keep some for themselves along the way, take the vicious path.

Bastiat wrote: "But how is this legal plunder to be identified? Quite simply. See if the law takes from some persons what belongs to them and gives it to other persons to whom it does not belong. See if the law benefits one citizen at the expense of another by doing what the citizen himself cannot do without committing a crime."[26] In other words, see if the law upholds privileges over rights, and plunder over property.

Capitalism, which is the only politico-economic system that upholds property rights consistently, is today being beset by ever more cronyism and privilege. If left un-righted, a populace that can no longer tell rights from privileges, and capitalism from cronyism and socialism, is eventually going to turn against the institution of private property as they witness ever more people acquiring wealth unjustly – a turn that will spell the end to rights-recognition. That terrible turn has happened before, and not so long ago, on a grand scale and to disastrous effect. The most notable example is Russia when it turned Bolshevik (Bolshevik means "majority"). That putsch, which resulted in the formation of the Union of Soviet Socialist Republics, was a bloody spectacle that took place during the world's most bloody war, with an even more bloody war and mass starvation following soon thereafter.

Mankind cannot afford to lose the most important lesson of the last century: liberty and private property rights are inextricably linked.

PROPERTY vs PLUNDER

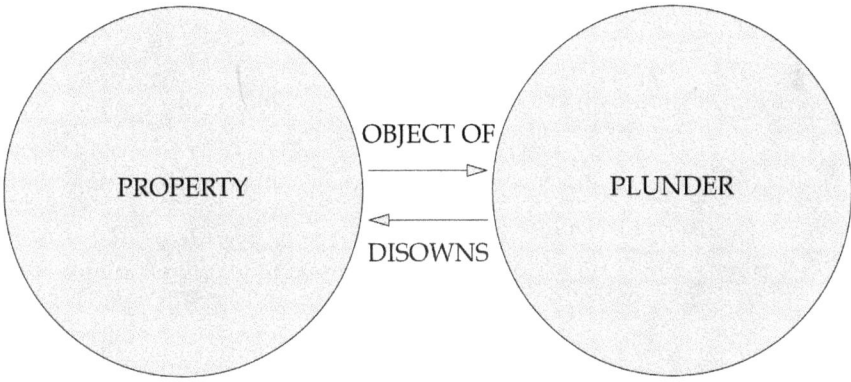

10. INDIVIDUAL RIGHTS vs. SO-CALLED COLLECTIVE "RIGHTS"

"Man holds these rights, not from the Collective nor for the Collective,
but against the Collective – as a barrier which the Collective cannot cross;
. . . these rights are man's protection against all other men."
Ayn Rand,
"Textbook of Americanism," (1962),
The Ayn Rand Column, **p83**

Only individuals have rights. A group or nation only has rights by metonymy. The rights of any group, including a nation, are in reality nothing more than the rights of the individuals comprising it, with the group acting as agent of its members with their consent (if it is a legitimate collective). If a group, such as a nation, claims "rights" over and above the rights held by its individual members, that is called collectivism.

What is promulgated today as "human rights" are for the most part not rights at all. Far from it. One does not have rights simply by belonging to the human species, which is a collectivist premise. Nor is there such a thing as "economic rights"; there is only political rights, being the

Rights of Man. It is only by being a man – a volitional reasoning being, or by being on the path to becoming a man, that rights-recognition is warranted, and then only if one is not violating or threatening to violate the rights of others.

Rights are not subject to vote, but privileges can be. A majority can impose its will on a minority through initiation of force, but it can never do so by right. A dictator can impose his or her will on a populace by force too, but again, cannot do so by right. Initiations of force are always by might, not right.

The Rights of Man is the only valid conception of rights. So-called collective rights, including "human rights," is the anti-concept of rights. Anti-concepts are "an artificial, unnecessary, and (rationally) unusable term, designed to replace and obliterate some legitimate concepts – a term which sounds like a concept, but stands for a 'package-deal' of disparate, incongruous, contradictory elements taken out of any logical conceptual order or context, a 'package-deal' whose (approximately) defining characteristic is always a non-essential. This last is the essence of the trick."[27]

So-called human rights usurp the Rights of Man by focusing on non-essentials. Those non-essentials include making the material requirements for human survival, comfort, even unearned dignity the subject of rights-claims, then mortgaging the lives of men of ability to supply those things to they who are unable or unwilling to earn them for themselves. The essential that needs to be focused on in order to arrive at legitimate rights is the reasoning mind and its existential needs, namely: moral space.

No group, including the human race, has the right to do what no individual man has the right to do, such as murder, enslave or steal. No person or group of persons has the right to violate individual rights, meaning the Rights of Man.

COLLECTIVISM vs INDIVIDUALISM

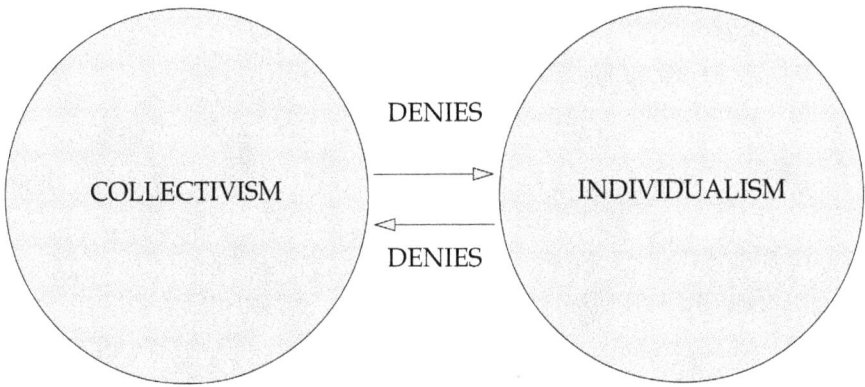

DENIES

COLLECTIVISM → INDIVIDUALISM

DENIES

11. SUMMARY AND CONCLUSION

"To respect individual rights may not be a sufficient condition for a moral life, but it certainly is a necessary condition."
Larry Sechrest
"Violence, Virtue and Vice,"
The Free Radical (June 2001), # 47, p32

Man is the living being who is able to reason, and who relies on reasoning to survive and flourish. Rights protect man's identity in a social context by defining and maximizing each and every man's moral space mutualistically. Moral space forms the social sphere in which men are free to reason and act on their reasoning. The universal maximization and mutualization of moral space, whereby every man enjoys autonomy, is called liberty.

A concise formulation of the concept of liberty was first recorded in Scripture two thousand years ago. Scripture prescribed liberty and called it "the perfect law."

The first comprehensive theory for rights and liberty was published only three centuries ago. Liberty was instituted (albeit imperfectly and inconsistently) by a nation for the first time a little more than two centuries ago. The corruption of the institution of rights and a systematic undermining of liberty began in earnest roughly one century ago. A complete loss of liberty and the destruction of the institution of rights is now imminent because of a lack of *agape*, which is the ethos of good-willed reasoning, and because of a prevalence of *philos*, the ethos of wantonly wishing and desiring.

Rights have been instituted for the tiniest of blips in human history, and only in a small corner of the globe at that. What remains of the discovery and institution of rights is a poor shadow of its former enlightened self, with privileges now being passed off as rights on an almost wholesale basis. If moral man is to survive, and humanity along with him and her, and if liberty is to be enjoyed, an enlightened concept of rights needs to be reinstituted as the unassailable moral currency of all politico-social interactions.

Gaining rights, which can only be done by and because of reason, is realized in five stages, with each stage denoting a specific sense of the word "have" in the claim "I/we have rights." The first is pre-realization, when rights are nothing more than a metaphysical imperative needing to be discovered: that the nature of being man necessitates him and her having moral space. The second is conceptually, when rights advance to being mental entities recognizing the metaphysical imperative. Those mental entities are the moral principles required to maximize moral space mutualistically. The third is effectually, when rights are backed by overwhelming retaliatory force should they be violated. The fourth is mutualistically, when rights are agreed to and form a relationship between enlightened men. The fifth is institutionally, when rights are formalized by being codified in law. Epistemologically, these five stages may be abbreviated to three: needing rights (stage one); having rights in mind (stage two), and; enjoying rights to varying degrees of universality and effectuality (stages three, four, and five).

Rights are fundamentally antithetical to privilege. The solution to the political and social problems of the world, now and always, is simple: remove privilege in all its forms. This can only be achieved if people stop asking their governments to initiate force on their behalf.

Rights are the only social contract that is consonant with justice, and more, that has good-willed reasoning as its ethos. It is only when rights are had in mind, meaning mentally grasped, that they can be enforced, mutualized, instituted, and ultimately enjoyed by all who would not violate them.

Capitalism is the means of instituting individualism, whereby every man lives for him or herself at no one's expense. Socialism is the means of instituting collectivism, which is the systematic violation of individual rights, whereby privileged members of a society get to live at the expense of the unprivileged.

Compossibility is a litmus test that can be used to determine whether a set of alleged rights is a legitimate set of rights or not. Today's governments are attempting to uphold a demonstrably incompossible set of "rights," the most notable being the Universal Declaration of Human Rights, which is a mishmash of rights and privileges. The UN's Universal Declaration of Human Rights is unsustainable because it contradicts and is incompatible with man's nature. It is incompatible with universal autonomy, with liberty, and with men being free to choose, act and take responsibility for their own choices and actions whilst living amongst other men. It is incompatible with maximizing moral space at no one's expense.

Grasping and respecting the rights of others as being no different to one's own is a responsibility that comes with having rights oneself. Rights permit no hypocrisy. Affording rights-recognition to those who do not yet grasp rights, but do not violate or threaten to violate rights, is a form of paying-it-forward that enables individuals to grow into rights and attain the stature of free men, while strengthening the institution of rights for everyone.

Most importantly, property rights are the only means of implementing rights. Upholding property rights ensures "that the effects of other people's foolishness and vice will be limited to their own domain,"[28] and that "a hopeless chaos of clashing views, interests, demands, desires, and whims" is avoided[29].

Distinguishing property from plunder is essential to a judicious recognition and application of rights. Property is synonymous with value-creation, and contrasts with possession of or dominion over free utility that is bereft of value. Value results from tradable enhancements being made to free utility because of human effort.

The core distinction between property and non-property is whether effort, and mental effort especially, has given rise to a thing's value, and specifically, how the elements of nature have been rearranged by effort, or a new application has been introduced, to produce that value.

Lastly, only individuals have rights. A group, whether it is a tribe, a nation, or the human race as a whole, has no more rights than the rights of the individual members comprising it. Any claim by a group, however large, over and above the rights of its individual members is a claim to privilege, which is the very antithesis of rights.

All of the above leads us to our conclusion: that the only legitimate function of government, which has a legal monopoly on the use of force, is to protect the rights of men, and that this is done by maximizing every man's moral space mutualistically. Government fails in its *raison d'etre* if it violates the rights of men in order to meet the material needs, or worse, the desires, of humans. Meeting the material needs or desires of humans should be left to the free market and to charity, which are both voluntary in nature. There is no moral justification for the existence of government other than to secure the Rights of Man.

CONDITIONS OF EXISTENCE REQUIRED FOR THE SURVIVAL OF MAN

AGAINST   FOR

PRIVILEGES
PLUNDER
PHILOS
COLLECTIVISM
IMMORAL SPACE
SOCIALISM
COERCION
SLAVERY

RIGHTS
PROPERTY
AGAPE
INDIVIDUALISM
MORAL SPACE
CAPITALISM
PERSUASION
LIBERTY

And that concludes this treatise on an objective philosophy of rights.

Now that you have completed Rights 101, take a moment to test yourself by completing the "Know Your Rights?" test online at www. rightsinstitute.org.

NOTES

[1] The original quote is, "Liberty without learning is always in peril, and learning without liberty is always in vain," from John F. Kennedy's Remarks in Nashville at the 90th Anniversary Convocation of Vanderbilt University on 18 May 1963.

[2] Ayn Rand, "Man's Rights" (1963), *The Virtue of Selfishness*, p93. This is the most concise definition of rights that is objective in its formulation.

[3] *A Universal Etymological Dictionary* by Nathan Bailey (1726, 1737, and 1775 editions). Also, *A General English Dictionary* by John Kersey (1708).

[4] *Nicomachean Ethics* I.13.

[5] See www.wikitionary.com. "Woke" denotes that state of sleepiness and semi-consciousness immediately after waking when one is neither fully awake nor fully asleep, as opposed to being "*a*wake" – literally "not woke" – which denotes being fully conscious and alert.

[6] Legal courtesies can and should be given to humans who have no possibility of ever reasoning to protect them against inhumane treatment and cruelty, but these courtesies may only be called rights metonymously. Rights are only ever exercised by reason, or through action that puts one on the path to reasoning.

[7] Ayn Rand, "Man's Rights" (1963), *The Virtue of Selfishness*, p110. Henry Hazlitt told Ayn Rand that Ludwig von Mises had referred to her as "the most courageous man in America", which reportedly

delighted her. See *Henry Hazlitt: Old Pro of Economic Journalism, An LR Interview* by Jeff Riggenbach, 1 October 1978.

[8] *Questions sur l'Encyclopédie* (1770-1774) in chapter titled "Canon Law: Ecclesiastical Ministry." An extrapolation on Aristotle's observation that "the virtues are modes of choice or involve choice." [Nicomachean Ethics, book 2, Chapter 5, 1106a2.]

[9] John Locke, *Second Treatise of Government* (1689), Chapter VI, Section 57.

[10] Leonardo da Vinci, Notebooks # 1204.

[11] Source: www.usdebtclock.org. Unfunded liabilities are debt obligations that do not have sufficient funds set aside to pay the debt. The figure at time of this work's publication is $124.5 trillion, growing at a rate of roughly $800 million per hour, or $5.70 per hour per taxpayer, every hour of every day.

[12] *The Virtue of Selfishness*, p112 and 113.

[13] Ayn Rand, Galt's Speech, *For The New Intellectual*, p182.

[14] Ayn Rand, Galt's Speech, *For The New Intellectual*, p135.

[15] Speech to the House of Commons, 22 October 1945.

[16] *The Free Radical*, Issue 77, (2007), p33.

[17] *The Merchant of Venice* (1596-1599), Act IV, Scene I.

[18] Ayn Rand, "Man's Rights" (1963), *The Virtue of Selfishness*, p. 94.

[19] Ayn Rand, "What is Capitalism?", *Capitalism: The Unknown Ideal*, p19.

[20] *Economic Harmonies* (1850), p205.

[21] *Economic Harmonies* (1850), p236.

[22] *Economic Harmonies* (1850), p27.

[23] *Knowledge and Decisions* (1980), p47.

[24] The balance scales in the diagram signifies that two parties in a voluntary trade trade with each other on equal terms and both derive value from the exchange, *not* that their trade results in an exchange of equal value.

[25] *Economic Harmonies* (1850), p236.

[26] *The Law*, p17.

[27] Ayn Rand, "'Extremism,' or The Art of Smearing," *Capitalism: The Unknown Ideal*, originally published in the September 1964 issue of *The Objectivist Newsletter*.

[28] Tibor Machan, *Classical Individualism*, p70.

[29] Ayn Rand, "The Cashing-In: The Student 'Rebellion,'" *Capitalism: The Unknown Ideal*, p259.

KNOW YOUR RIGHTS? TEST

Select ONE answer per question:

1. Rights originate as:
   a) Claims to having one's material needs satisfied
   b) Conditions that guarantee universal human dignity
   c) A requirement of reason and morality in a social context

2. Rights are realized as:
   a) The will of the majority
   b) What is set forth in the Universal Declaration of Human Rights
   c) Principles that define and maximize moral space

3. Rights are gained by and because of:
   a) Reason
   b) Passing laws
   c) Possessing the human genome

4. Respecting rights is a:
   a) Necessary condition for a moral life
   b) Sufficient condition for a moral life
   c) Neither of the above

5. Indispensable for protecting and implementing the right to disagree is:
   a) Property rights
   b) Democracy
   c) Free speech laws

6. In a society, rights are necessary for:
   a) Men to live as men
   b) Children to develop into men
   c) Both of the above

7. For the greatest chance of rights being enjoyed by all who would not violate them, their recognition must be:
   a) Reciprocated where possible
   b) Paid forward where affordable
   c) Both of the above

8. Rights are necessarily:
   a) Compatible with the nature of man
   b) Compossible with every other right
   c) Both of the above

9. Which of the following statements is true:
   a) Truth is a type of right
   b) Rights are a type of principle
   c) Principles are a type of right

10. Rights are limited to:
   a) Whatever the majority agrees are rights
   b) Any action that does not initiate or threaten to initiate force against others
   c) What is written in the Bill of Rights

11. The solution to problems that arise from the initiation of government force is:
    a) To pass laws that prevent those problems
    b) For everyone to stop asking governments to initiate force on their behalf
    c) There is no solution

12. We all have a right to:
    a) Food and shelter
    b) Not have our property taken from us
    c) Both of the above

13. Who should be recognized as having a full set of rights:
    a) All humans
    b) All men who do not violate or threaten to violate rights
    c) Only moral men

14. Which of the following statements is true:
    a) Basic rights are positive (i.e., oblige action)
    b) Basic rights are negative (i.e., oblige inaction)
    c) Both of the above

15. Politics, at its root, is the struggle between:
    a) The left and the right
    b) The individual and the state
    c) Those wanting privileges and/or those wanting rights

16. Privileges:
    a) Are types of rights
    b) Violate rights
    c) Complement rights

17. The only way to implement rights is through:
    a) Property rights
    b) Sensible legislation
    c) Dialogue and compromise

18. Forcing others to act in accordance with your own will causes them to act:
    a) Amorally
    b) Immorally
    c) Morally

19. The ultimate source of property is:
    a) Physical labor
    b) The creative, valuing mind
    c) Scarcity

20. All property comprises:
    a) Valuable effort
    b) Tradable utility
    c) Both of the above

21. Free utility leading to effortless living is a product of:
    a) Nature's bounty
    b) Expired property
    c) Both of the above

22. The principal effect of upholding rights is to institute:
    a) Moral space
    b) Equality
    c) Fairness

23. Moral space is the sphere in which everyone:
    a) Is free to be moral
    b) Is free to be immoral
    c) Both of the above

24. What makes members of a society fit for liberty?
    a) Agape
    b) Diversity
    c) Equality

25. Liberty is autonomy for:
    a) All at the expense of none
    b) Some at the expense of some
    c) All at the expense of some

26. A group has the right to initiate force against individuals:
    a) Never
    b) So long as the majority agrees
    c) So long as the majority benefits

27. The essence of the welfare state is:
    a) Charity
    b) Plunder
    c) Justice

28. Charity is giving that is:
    a) Voluntary
    b) Coercive
    c) Both of the above

29. Nazi Germany and the USSR were both:
    a) Socialist
    b) Capitalist
    c) Neither socialist nor capitalist

30. The United States today is:
    a) Capitalist
    b) Socialist
    c) A mixed economy

31. Socialism is a politico-economic system where men deal with one another by:
    a) Persuasion
    b) Force

32. Capitalism is a politico-economic system where men deal with one another by:
    a) Persuasion
    b) Force

33. Injustice necessarily involves:
    a) Rights being violated
    b) Some people being better off than others
    c) Laws being broken

34. The only legitimate function of government is to uphold the rights of:
    a) The majority
    b) Minorities
    c) The individual

35. What does Scripture conclude about liberty:
    a) That it is contrary to God's will
    b) That it is the perfect law and should be instituted
    c) Nothing

36. The responsibility that comes with having rights oneself is:
    a) To be one's brothers' keeper
    b) Not to violate or threaten to violate anyone's rights
    c) There are no responsibilities

HAVING READ OUR TREATISE, YOU ARE NOW INVITED TO BECOME A MEMBER OF RIGHTS INSTITUTE™. TO BECOME A MEMBER AND RECEIVE A FREE CERTIFICATE OF MEMBERSHIP CONFIRMING THAT YOU ARE PROFICIENT IN YOUR KNOWLEDGE OF THE PHILOSOPHY OF RIGHTS, SUBMIT YOUR TEST RESULTS ONLINE AT: www.rightsinstitute.org

ENQUIRIES CAN BE SENT TO THE AUTHOR THROUGH THE CONTACT US PAGE ON THE RIGHTS INSTITUTE WEBSITE

PURSUIT OF HAPPINESS

LIFE

LIBERTY

ONE MAN WITH
COURAGE MAKES
A MAJORITY

Pictured: Hercules Capturing Cerberus, by Lorenzo Mattielli.
Hercules is shown triumphant as he completes his Twelfth Labor.
Quote is a paraphrase of the following one attributed to
Andrew Jackson, seventh president of the United States:
"Desperate courage makes One a majority."
Design copyright Inspirationz Inc. Limited.
Artwork by Ira Paniukova.

www.ingramcontent.com/pod-product-compliance
Lightning Source LLC
Chambersburg PA
CBHW072153020426
42334CB00018B/1993